POLITICAL SUBJECT

POLITICAL SUBJECT

Caleb Beckwith

ROOF BOOKS
NEW YORK

ISBN: 978-1-93182-90-3

Library of Congress Control Number: 2018957717

NEW YORK STATE OF OPPORTUNITY | Council on the Arts This book is made possible, in part, by the New York State Council on the Arts with the support of Governor Andrew Cuomo and the New York State Legislature.

Roof Books
are published by
Segue Foundation
300 Bowery, New York, NY 10012
seguefoundation.com

Roof Books
are distributed by
Small Press Distribution
1341 Seventh Street
Berkeley, CA. 94710-1403
800-869-7553 or spdbooks.org

for my friends—thos kids sens

Contents

Political Subject

ACCELERATIONIST RENAISSANCE

raw dog
canon formation

anointed aphasic
flat earth undercurrent

tortured sense
correct and unconscionable

MUTUAL AID

on the hook
confirmation bias

immaterial outdoor
affection

by crook, please
somebody

GLOSS

antifa
matte

trauma
palate

by all
means

HEGEMONIC DYSPHORIA

polyphonic homology
mask up

blockbuster
cement truck

reverse orgone
hard drive

DIALECTICIANS

a certain
curtain

SHADE

front
line

human
microphone

nirvana
unplugged

COMMIE CAMP

no
culture
save
pop
culture

COHERENCE

identified

BLACK BLOC IN THE NATION
OR, THE MATERIALISTS

going
out
of
business
american
apparel
40%
off

POPULAR AFFRONT

counterfactual
tensile

biological
turnstile

general affectation
let's go dutch

BROKEN WINDOWS

tired repetition
fluorescent endocrine

prone to
fits of abyss

it's
spring

THEY LIVE

rugged
data entry

embroiled
compost

dearth struck
shiver of invention

MASKING AGENT

lapidary
simulacra

displaced
nostalgia

somebody
stop me

PATH OF LEAST RESISTANCE

amiable
supervillain

pugnacious
observation

come at
me, bro

NEWBIE'S LAMENT

bayside story
salon tan

tastes like soap
enough at least

fled destruction
spoiled flesh

SEASONAL DEPRESSION

amazon
sold
out
of
1984
in
three
hours
cashier
said
this
is
how
revolutions
start

ORGANIZATIONAL PSYCHOLOGY

healthy
self-esteem

cautious
optimism

belabored
consensus

FLAKE

oh
yes
I
was
one

I LOVE THE RESISTANCE!

half
life

relief
valve

diet
gnosticism

GOOD GUYS

double layer
spam folder

police grade
trip sitter

I'm complicit
get me out of here!

DESPERATE TIMES

real life
rally cap

measured
in a vacuum

skull tattoo
is also something

ALLY COMPLEX

college
radio

dj
abstraction

blissful
condition

FRICTIONLESS DIFFERENCE
OR, PEACEFUL PROTEST

dogpark
paradise

headlamp
gaslight

wait
your turn

AFFILIATION

lights
out

knee
deep

punch
line

AESTHETICS

even
a
cavern
of
caverns
can
sound
appealing
after
a while

UTOPIA

epic
withdraw

ecstatic
insecurity

suspended from
class consciousness

TOLERANCE

yogic
endurance

free
for all

silent
but deadly

WHITE FEMINISM

ethical
pink
eye

GENTILITY

no
thank
you
man

HOMOSOCIALITY

poison
pill

razzle
berry

dude
ranch

EMBODIMENT

bottom
text

down
side

brutal
look

GENDER

check
please

MASCULINITY

in
retrograde

CONVICTION

the
kind
of
guy
who
will
always
have
one
more
beer

REALISTIC DEMANDS

birds of
unfettered

pragmatism
agile

as excuse
I'll take it

CONTINUITY

self-help
standoff

get out
alive

I mean
now

MIRROR STAGE

antimicrobial
ego deflation

encampment
procedure upended

citronella candle
fruit of the gods

NOSTALGIA

armchair professional
friendly outfit

depressed value
irrational confidence

systemic clarity
astral projection

ECONOMIC REALISM

gold dust
hangover cure

interview
on ice

stay salty
my friends

STREET SMARTS

tout court
employment aegis

rigid fuck
boy patrol

c'mon you're
hurting the movement

SOLIDARITY

peach
state

green
day

long
division

COGNITIVE LABOR

weathered honeymoon
savings account

intestinal flora
lizard brain

9-5 decline
anytime, buddy

FATIGUE

dissociated
state

of
affairs

big league
wax museum

STRIVING

love song
insecure attachment

mindfully
overwhelmed

always a wave
never outright

CRITICISM

righteous shame
interlocutor special

literally sat
around the house

neurotypical implosion
sounds true

WELLNESS

dulcet toning
precarity trigger

ergonomic
SCOBY hotel

late-late
pullover season

READING

is
it
over
yet?

SUNSET

last generation
beach house

tired
sublime

credit repair
horizon line

TACT

assisted
living

playoff
weekend

sink or
swim scene

MEMOIR

hot garbage
stress test

close up
reflex

safe bet
more or less

SOCIALIZATION

shoreline or
shipwreck

erstwhile
friendship

psychogeography
isn't real

FACE OFF

synchronic
hullabaloo

gentrified
haircut

bank shot
revenge

PERSISTENCE

austerity
magazine

tremor
control

not your druthers
punching bag

RUNNING DIALOG

good
tilt

sustainable
polemic

empty calorie
die hard

STARTER PACK

modern box
low block

disabused tender
negativity

adaptation
or oversight?

ABOVE THE FRAY

trickle down
discourse

never ending
transplant

male lesbian
separatist syndrome

CRYSTAL LIGHT

vulgar
primrose

sebaceous
feeder road

no thanks
in a nutshell

EMPIRICISM

port of call
woke daddy

pell mell stay
glow twang

cultural ice wall
over the top

GUILTY PLEASURE

virtue
signal

ride
share

drive
thru

PARADIGM

up
on
us
all

GET OUT

pregnant
horror
dead
on
arrival

LOVE WITCH

blitzed
bandwidth

ironic
distance

nihilism's
escape hatch

PROPRIETARY DESERT

gingham beach
fantasy cover

indefinite on
brand craving

genre piece
de resistance

MELTDOWN

anthropocene
night life

reproductive
boredom

erotic rewards
card

ACCOUNTABILITY

deep
thaw

run
off

come
thru

INTENTION

well
meaning
melee

SEAT AT THE TABLE

greatest
hits
live

IDENTITY

finally
some
body
gets
me

BIG DATA

why
no
I
don't
have
plans
on
friday

BLOWOUT

body
conscious

hedge
fund

prolonged
determinism

EMOTIONAL CALCULUS

aesthetic essentialism
basketball courage

dank method
toe ring

stop it—you're
embarrassing me

MICROWAVE

western
edition

cognizant
militant

as above
blows

FASHION FORWARD

intemperate
trench coat

grey sheen
weathervane

no
dice

CALIFORNIA

is
no
escape

AWARE

I'd
rather
not
be

HUMAN CAPITAL

sabbatical

FIGHT OR FLIGHT

slapstick
tremor

serious
dilemma

obscurant baptism
all at once

WE GET IT

shit
stirring

scare
mongering

skull
duggery

DISCOURSE

communal obligation
intense recognition

historical coincidence
provisional clarity

ambulance chaser
kegstand

OUT OF STEP

with
the
world

REPORTAGE

tearing up
download

abiding beef
big feelings

who wore
it better?

COMING OF AGE

uncultured fandom
scathed vitriol

staunch monogamist
revolutionary defeatism

help me
help myself

MIDDLE CLASS

hefty lite
retirement fund

self-exculpation
tract

dead or alive
beach volleyball

PROGRESS

invidious demands
someone else's plans

assertively neutral
enlightenment scar

fully automated
necessity

RENT CONTROL

carnal affluence
survivor's guilt

greek row
love affair

terms
of surrender

LUCKY DOG

laboring
in
the
last
days
of
the
english
department

BASKETBALL

as
the
game
went
on
my
hands
hurt

I THINK

good
grief

FIT

to
be
tired

ANACHRONISM'S DELIGHT

sliding doors
social drag

instrumental
life troll

welcome home
irrationality

WALLOW

in
self
regard

ALWAYS

time
to
reify

SUBJECTION

kiss
cam

rip
tide

what
ever

HISTORY

glacial
indifference

separation
anxiety

ask me about
my privilege

LET'S ROLL

glad
hand

shock
troops

good
bye

DEBT

phatic
confession

long in
the tooth

your scholarship
is showing

ACHIEVEMENT

come
again?

TEARS OF APOLLO

favorite son
investment parade

a borderline
brewski affair

usually they
fall down now

MUSHROOM CLOUD

altered
states

SCIENCE FICTION

in
flight

world
building

enough
already

NO BRAINER

I remember

AVANT GARDE

bad ass
overhead

divine creative
cloud

I'm giving the
orders now

MUSEUM OF CAPITALISM

partial
critique

WANNABE

yours
truly

POLITICAL SUBJECT

matter
of
fact

SICK PAY

kickflip
revenue

PAID VACATION

forbidden island
galaxy cruise

appropriate means
of consumption

intestinal terraforming
as ethical frontier

LIBIDINAL ECONOMY

pop tantra respect-
ability goggles

ride or die
protocol

take it
sleazy

SENTIMENTAL JOURNEY

hermetic
burner unit

upper crust
avocado toast

my rent control
for a water hose

SUPPER

structure

MONDAYS

are
the
cruelest
month

INDULGENCE

total
sin tax

screen free
sunday

I don’t even know
you anymore

INCREMENTALISM

belated matrix
antinatalist outfit

gravedigger or
gay parade?

asking for
an enemy

LEAN IN

reality augmentation
apocrypha pedal

abiding condescension
technocratic blues

ikea moment
failing upward

SOUL SEARCHING

spiritual industry
thought leader

caddy corner
file path

gremlins in
the system

CULTURE INDUSTRY

arcane telepathy
research forest

algorithmic legibility
middlebrow motif

everyone's favorite
pee paw

CAREER SUICIDE

observational
criteria rub

concern trolling
alternator

looks like a
loner to me

COST

of
living
increase

PARTIAL

radical wellness
irony poisoning

navel gaze
haze pro

how art
thou?

THINGY

prefigurative mulch
facial recognition

naive reaction
cauliflower ear

frightened contemplation
necessary excess

COUNTERCULTURAL EDGE

content velocity
thirst trap

pretty green
legacy hire

return of
the rat

TOXICITY

system
of
a
downer

ABETTORS

go
on
tell
me
you
don't

FUGUE STATE

alter ego
pep talk

makes imprint
rehearsal handbag

a rescue
remedy occasion

ZEN DEVIL

present moment
headbang anthem

rewire your
brain

on and
off again

WORK

is
my
daddy

FANCY

a
noise
aficionado

STAY LOOSE

minimum viable
product placement

full throated
friendliness

business
as usual

BAD CITIZEN

are
you
my
neighbor?

NEVER FORGET

scratch made
waking nap

distributed
work force

soylent
super soldier

LONE WOLF

epigenetic
particular animus

bad vibes
allergy pill

free flowing
swan dive

PAY IT FORWARD

taut
body

culture
vulture

ideas of
reference

BLANK CHECK

digital native
buzz word

pacific strength
aphorism

the pleasure
of withdraw

BEHAVIORAL THERAPY

socially invested
restricted area

memento mori
cleansing

burning the candle
at both ends

DEJA VU

irreverent
compliment

psychic
recalcitrance

different in nature
not degree

COTERIE

was
an
inside
job

GUILTY MIND

holiday
body treat

monocultural
playpen

some of us
live here

GOBBLE

gobble

DEATH WISH

memory squat
hype machine

psycho
catastrophe

bare witness
bloodsport

ALTRUISM

frugal fun
apology tour

soft
structural good

tender hearted
social laboratory

THIRTY

teenage
strength

blurb
thirst

I have
some

LIBERAL ARTS

bumbling stop
zine warfare

helmet
hair raiser

misery of
the cohort

SOCIAL PRACTICE

forgotten
namesake

twee castle
incarnate

object lesson
explode

GENERATIONAL WEALTH

toxic
accumulation

choker on
the mainstream

a killer
in the woods

CASUAL

authentic
reproduction chic

fancy free
nouveau riche

everyone loves
a happy ending

FREE PASS

bottle
neck

PANIC ATTACK

finally

END OF HISTORY

redoux

I TRIED

passionate marriage
overton window

fatal flaw
aesthetic precarity

back on
my bullshit

NO FUTURE

peace

California,

DEATH VALLEY

acute energy
zodiac efficiency

fermentation landlord
maximalist key

inverse ambition
gentrification tax

low key eddie
bauer edition

emissions restriction
eucalyptus mound

healthy enterprise
natural lighting

hot tub
sanctuary city

sliding scale
wait list

gaslight
fuel cell

art house
skills manual

displaced pedestrian
insight

layoff paranoia
video tutorial

private garage
tipping point

pace and space
support line

online exclusive
lifestyle brand

class traitor
google doc

life hack
privacy guard

slow and low
lifestyle creep

climate control
cultural capital

morning jaunt
dynamic palliative

white vanguard
property swarm

truck nuts
canopy mirage

aural induced
psychological flexibility

open source
alumni association

mauve obsessed
bass lick

tremor control
dictation software

zen center
realtor bump

cosmic exfoliation
lived flatness

PLANET FITNESS

peak performance
body shame

remote control
gentry threshold

critical mass
market icon

fossil fuel
heat check

prime day
jock itch

sans serif
start up

big box
climbing lunch

single speed
payroll ratio

yoga star
man child

high octane
third way

TREASURE ISLAND

resistant
gradation
consensus

unwound
alterity
wound

tripartite
bumpkin
logic

gender
neutral
balkanization

cove
mentality
feedback

real
purchase
mandate

lazy
haymaker
river

taxed
imposter
syndrome

competitive
brat
model

redemption
narrative
mechanism

hippie
software
update

just
parlance
parade

creative
generational
debt

eroded
play
station

wellness
key
note

dialectical
coping
skills

stigmatized
depth
perception

hailing
back
matter

generic
content
mine

unleashed
allergy
awareness

geologic
time
card

imperial
air
conditioning

every
man
date

adjunct
hell
bent

sovereign
land
mine

scarcity
fad
diet

with
holding
company

site
specific
fetish

electric
car
aura

second
wind
stream

self
discovery
channel

plur
beach
patrol

week
end
theory

real
luxury
experience

GRASS VALLEY

hard

water

damage

control

top

down

low

country

boy

cut

throat

coat

tail

spin

off

brand

new

blue

jean

tyranny

machine

wash

board

based

life

guide

book

club

kid

friendly

fire

squad

goal

keeper

play

time

share

sell

through

line

paper

trail

mix

tape

craft

work

boot

lick
job
list
serv
safe
space
program
hour
over
draft
dodger
game
theory
head
shot
time
log
jam
band
half
man
made
long
way
home

CALIFORNIA,

california,
nice to know ya

high time
I water the begonias

lest you pony
up a crew

repay each
implicit due

temperate as you
are blue

awash with
boyish mildew

I cordoned you off
from south cascadia

thinking we'd steal
away together

your honey weighed
upon my brow

furrowed now
like a furloughed cow

depression writ large
upon my heart

cast off home
like an old hair part

I won't budge
lest properly shoved

don't judge my love
till you've lugged my grudge

aged, abated, waylaid
full of so much hate

deign to cry
every time you try

could I
just die

for a slice
of pecan pie—

what's another couple years
dripping in the clear?

all that's here, well
worn like sheer

nothing left to fear
a new nadir

I miss my mother
I miss my father

I even miss
our idle prattle

time to shatter the
proverbial pancake batter

so what if life's a glass
of chardonnay?

it's still a gas
living by the bay

no city matches
caring complicity

urbane simplicity
pronounced erotic electricity

though it may not be easy
to find an authentic eatery

rest assured the sleazy
leave queasy

subject
to righteous teasing

legs astride, charm akimbo
smelling of wine and breath mints

this boondoggle
bobbles burritos

looking like
a malnourished flamingo

prone to paroxysms
sweeping solipsisms

acculturation becomes coastal
smoking cessation

ritual sublation begets
communal representation

collective identification
on a staycation

take it from
me, buddy

the bay bridge
blows easy

begrudging only
temerity

endearing everlasting
solidarity

ad infinitum
equanimity

Acknowledgments

Drafts of these poems were published in *ARMED CELL* and *ELDERLY*. Thanks to Brian Ang, Turner Canty, Jacob Kahn, Trisha Low, and Jamie Townsend for hosting this work as curators; to Brandon Brown, Mark Johnson, Christopher Nelms, Syd Staiti, and Suzanne Stein for their attention and encouragement as readers; to Kim Calder, Housten Donham, Gordon Faylor, Eddie Hopely, Liz Kinnamon, and Kate Robinson for their daily attention to any number of these drafts; and to Kate Robinson, again, for everything.